實用中文系列

# Chinese for Children
## COLORING/ACTIVITY BOOK

著色★連連看★記憶遊戲★等等‧‧‧

王 姚 文 編寫　by Wendy Lin

版權所有　不准翻印

copyright © 2002

CREATIVE WORLD ENT., INC.
43 Candlewick Court, Matawan, New Jersey 07747
(732)441-1704　　wang07747@yahoo.com.tw

All rights Reserved.
No part of this book may be reproduced or copied in any form,
or by any means, without permission.

ISBN 0-9715058-7-X

# Introduction

"Chinese for Children" is specially designed for the young native speakers of English who are learning verbal usage in Mandarin and who have little or no previous experience in learning Chinese. This book provides various activities such as coloring, word puzzle, and cut and paste to help expand daily vocabulary usage for younger children. They will find learning the Chinese language is not as difficult as they thought. Some children may enjoy the learning activities without help from others; however, most children may need adult help with English expressions. For this age child, we do not recommend written exercises. This book is basically to enforce the verbal and reading abilities. For writing enforcement they can start with Level I of **"The Effective Way of Learning Reading, Writing, and Speaking Chinese"** (More information about this series of books is listed on the back of this book.) If any child finds a particular activity too difficult, suggest moving on to another.

In order to help the children study independently, all the vocabulary use two different pronunciations. The one listed on the right side of each character is called "BoPoMoFo" which has been used in Taiwan. The other one is called pinyin which is listed under each character and has been used in mainland China since the 1960s. More information about *pinyin* can be found in Level One of **"The Effective Way of Learning Reading, Writing, and Speaking Chinese"**. (*Audio tapes are also available.*)

## ▶ 前　言 ◀

【兒童中文】主要是為以英文為母語的小孩而設計。培養他們學習中文的興趣，本書以各種生動活潑的方式介紹生字生詞，使孩子們在遊戲中學習，不但趣味十足，而且簡單容易，不僅適合以英文為母語的小孩，甚至華裔可同時學習中英雙語。對於年紀較小的孩子，英文閱讀能力有限，須要大人從旁解說，如果孩子本身已具備基本的英文閱讀能力，則可讓他們自做練習。本書設計主要針對幼兒，因此基本上不鼓勵寫字練習，而是專注於口語和識字的訓練。同時本書設計重點完全以趣味性為出發點，如果小孩在某個部份學習感到困難，不妨移到下一個練習。至於寫字練習可參考【實用中文】系列書（簡介列於本書後面），該系列書從第一冊開始即有初級寫字練習。

為養成孩子獨立學習習慣，生字除標以注音符號外並附有漢語拼音。漢語拼音未標示聲調，乃希望學習者以國字為主，選擇漢語拼音旨在輔助以英文為母語的孩子發音，雖然老師或家長與孩子一同標聲調也是學習活動之一，但是基于本書使用者年齡較小，因此並不鼓勵太早辨識聲調變化。

有關漢語拼音的詳細規則介紹，可參考【實用中文】系列書第一冊。【實用中文】系列書內容綱要簡介附在本書最後。

# Contents

Fruit, Colors, & Numbers ·················································· 1

Body Parts ·················································· 22

My Outfit ·················································· 42

Answers ·················································· 63

Index ·················································· 66

# Fruit, Colors, & Numbers

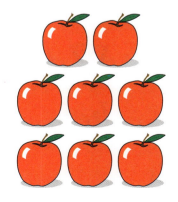

# numbers 數ㄕㄨ 字ㄗˋ
*shu  zi*

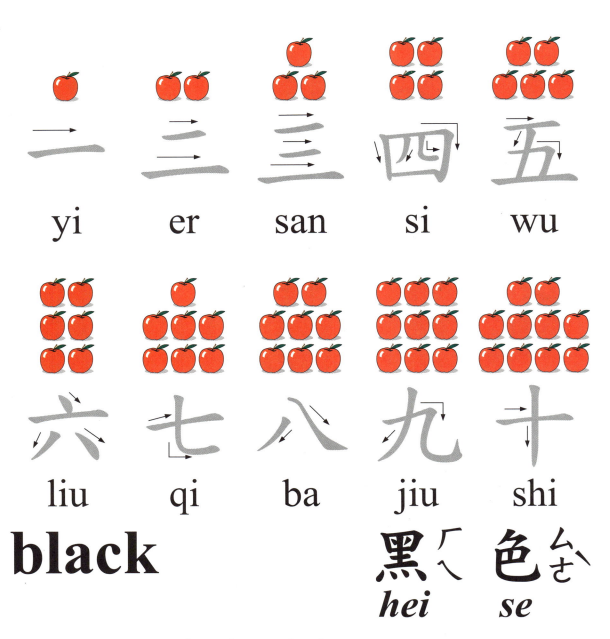

yi　er　san　si　wu

liu　qi　ba　jiu　shi

# black 黑ㄏㄟ 色ㄙㄜˋ
*hei  se*

*Trace the* 數字 黑色

# Write the number to match with each number of fruit.

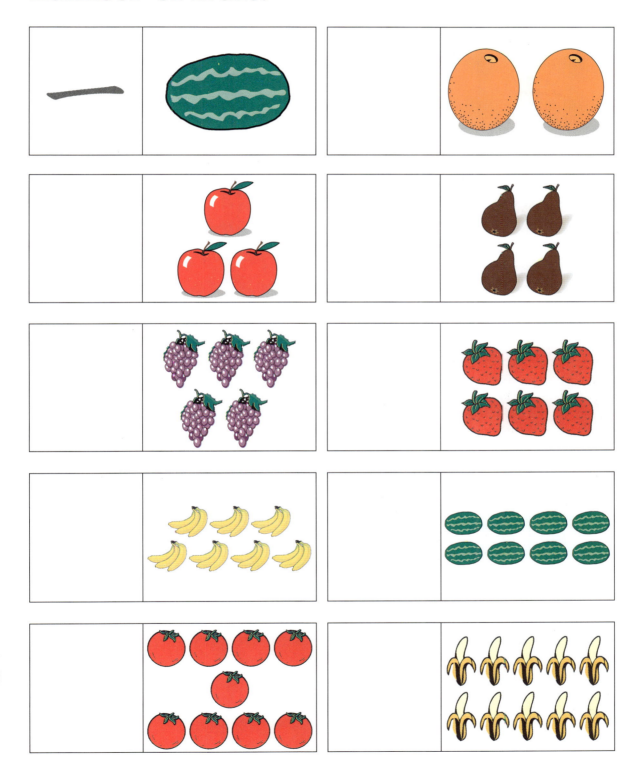

# Circle the number of fruit according to the number given.

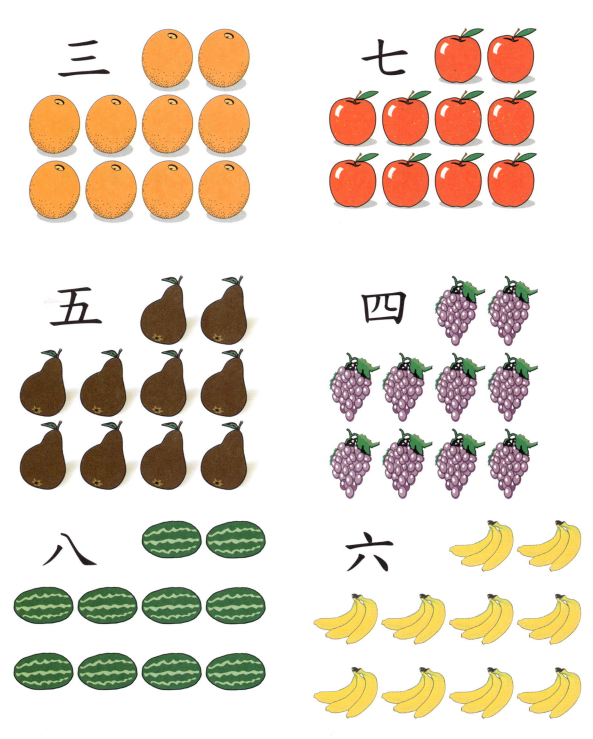

# Count the pictures and draw a circle around the right number.

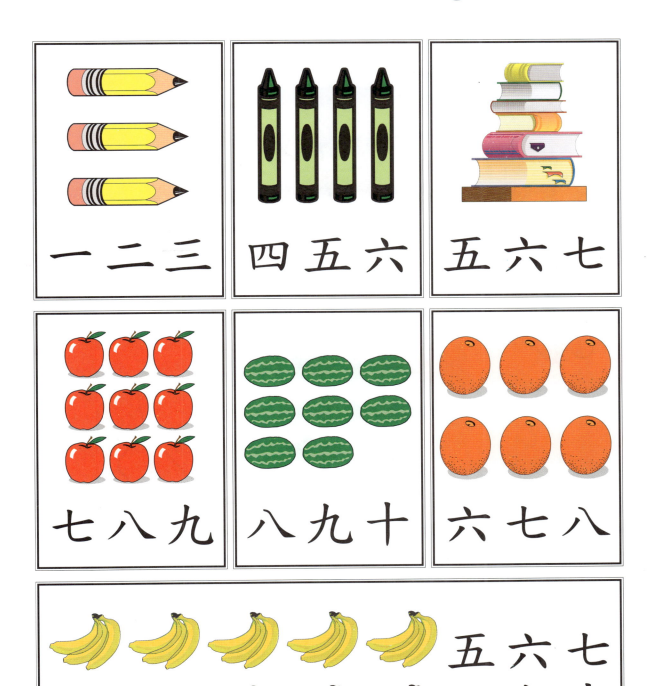

# CONNECT THE DOTS
## from 1 to 10

字 ㄗˋ
zi

character

apple 蘋ㄆㄧㄥˊ 果ㄍㄨㄛˇ
*Ping guo*

red color 紅ㄏㄨㄥˊ 色ㄙㄜˋ
*Hong se*

*Color the* 蘋果紅色

**banana** 香ㄒㄧㄤ 蕉ㄐㄧㄠ
Xiang jiao

**yellow color** 黃ㄏㄨㄤˊ 色ㄙㄜˋ
Huang se

*Color the* 香蕉黃色

# orange

桔ㄐㄩˊ子ㄗ˙
*Ju zi*

## orange color

桔ㄐㄩˊ紅ㄏㄨㄥˊ色ㄙㄜˋ
*Ju hong se*

*Color the* 桔子 桔紅色

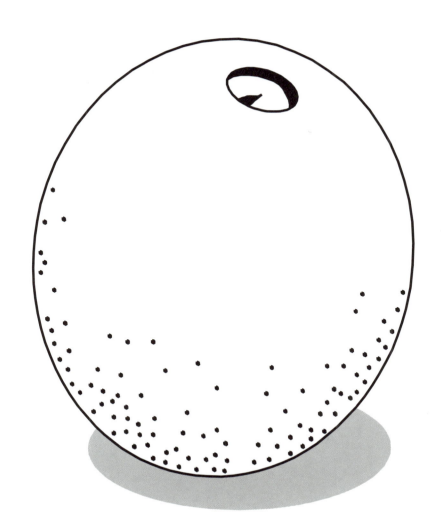

grapes 葡ㄆㄨˊ 萄ㄊㄠˊ
*Pu* *tao*

purple color 紫ㄗˇ 色ㄙㄜˋ
*zi* *se*

*Color the* 葡萄紫色

**watermelon** 西 瓜
Xi gua

**green color** 綠 色
lü se

*Color the* 西瓜綠色

# blueberries 藍ㄌㄢˊ莓ㄇㄟˊ
*Lan mei*

# blue color 藍ㄌㄢˊ色ㄙㄜˋ
*lan se*

*Color the* 藍莓藍色

# pear 梨ㄌㄧˊ子ㄗ
*Li  zi*

# brown color 咖ㄎㄚ啡ㄈㄟ色ㄙㄜˋ
*ka  fei  se*

*Color the* 梨子咖啡色

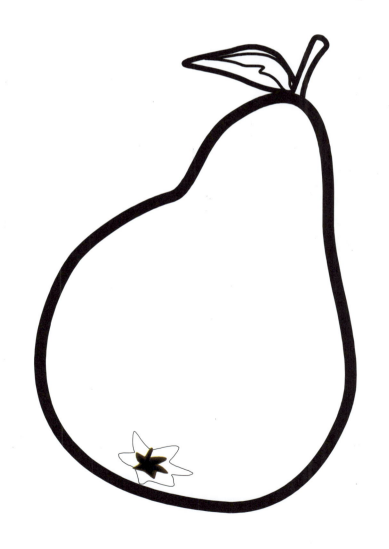

# Match the words to the fruit.

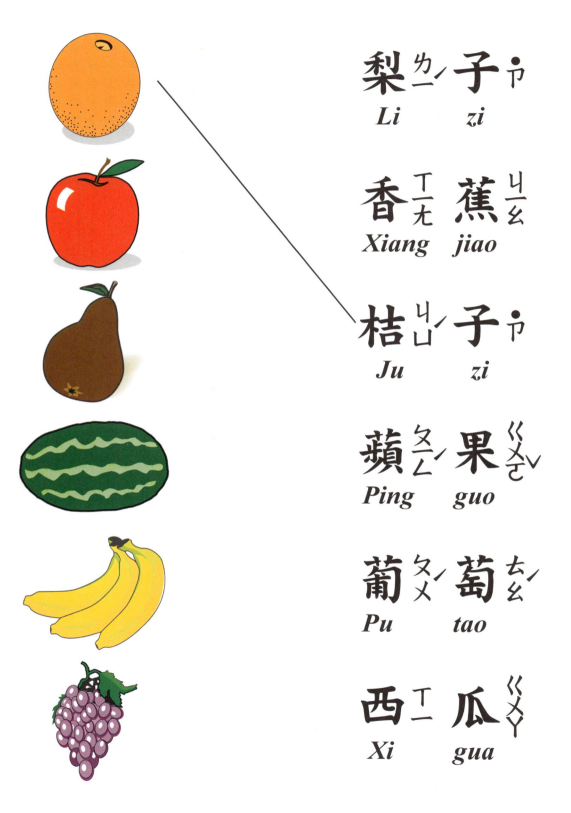

# Match the color to the fruit.

咖ㄎㄚ 啡ㄈㄟ 色ㄙㄜ
*ka   fei   se*

綠ㄌㄩ 色ㄙㄜ
*lü   se*

紅ㄏㄨㄥˊ 色ㄙㄜ
*hong   se*

桔ㄐㄩ 紅ㄏㄨㄥˊ 色ㄙㄜ
*ju   hong   se*

黃ㄏㄨㄤ 色ㄙㄜ
*huang   se*

紫ㄗˇ 色ㄙㄜ
*zi   se*

# Color by number

一：紅色　　　　二：紫色　　　　三：黃色
四：桔紅色　　　五：黑色　　　　六：藍色

**Look at the picture and read the words aloud.** *When you think you can remember them all turn to the next page.*

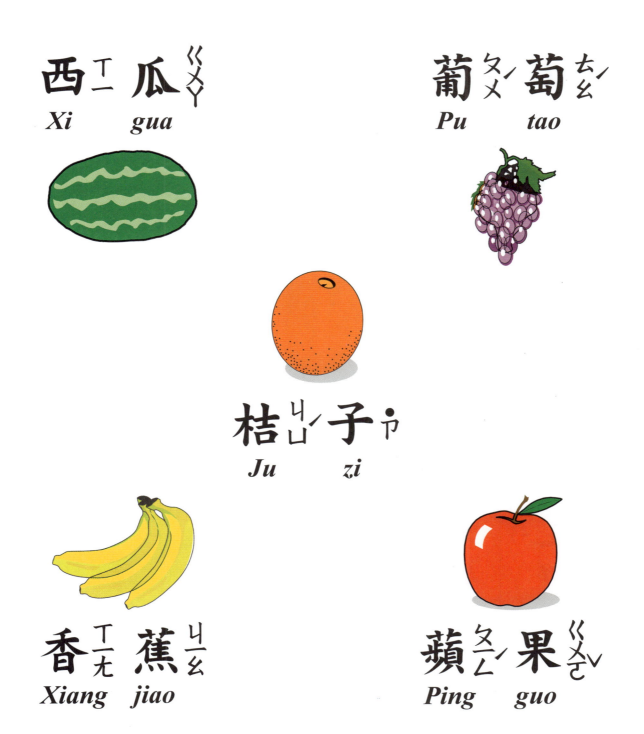

**Find the fruits you saw on the page before. Circle them.**

葡ㄆㄨˊ 萄ㄊㄠˊ
*Pu    tao*

西ㄒㄧ 瓜ㄍㄨㄚ
*xi    gua*

香ㄒㄧㄤ 蕉ㄐㄧㄠ
*xiang  jiao*

梨ㄌㄧˊ 子ㄗ
*li    zi*

木ㄇㄨˋ 瓜ㄍㄨㄚ
*mu    gua*

蘋ㄆㄧㄥˊ 果ㄍㄨㄛˇ
*ping   guo*

藍ㄌㄢˊ 莓ㄇㄟˊ
*lan   mei*

桔ㄐㄩˊ 子ㄗ
*ju    zi*

# Cut and Paste

Cut out the pictures on the bottom of this page and paste them into the right boxes in the puzzle.

| 西瓜 *xi gua* | 梨子 *li zi* | 葡萄 *Pu tao* |
|---|---|---|
| 蘋果 *Ping guo* | 香蕉 *Xiang jiao* | 木瓜 *mu gua* |
| 桔子 *Ju zi* | 藍莓 *lan mei* | 水果 *shui guo* |

19

# Can you help the monkey find the 香蕉？

*Circle each fruit in the same order as it is in the box below to find the path.*

西瓜 → 桔子 → 藍莓 → 蘋果 →
桔子 → 梨子 → 西瓜 → 葡萄 →
梨子 → 蘋果

# Below is a list of words hiding in the puzzle. Find them and circle them.

(Words can only be read from left to right or from top to bottom.)

| 七 | 瓜 | 二 | 果 | 葡 | 莓 | 西 |
|---|---|---|---|---|---|---|
| 籃 | 莓 | 蘋 | 四 | 萄 | 草 | 六 |
| 西 | 瓜 | 果 | 萄 | 藍 | 莓 | 三 |
| 五 | 色 | 紅 | 十 | 色 | 黑 | 白 |
| 桔 | 紅 | 色 | 八 | 九 | 色 | 梨 |
| 子 | 綠 | 色 | 咖 | 啡 | 色 | 子 |

1. Watermelon
2. Apple
3. Grapes
4. Blueberry
5. Red color
6. Blue color
7. Black color
8. Orange color
9. Orange
10. Pear
11. Borwn color
12. Green color
13. Ten
14. Eight
15. Seven

# Body Parts

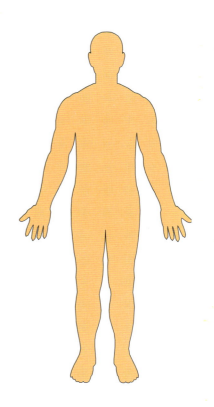

# eye

# 眼睛
*Yan jing*

*Color the* 眼睛藍色

# mouth

嘴 ㄗㄨㄟˇ 巴 ㄅㄚ
zui ba

*Color the* 嘴巴紅色

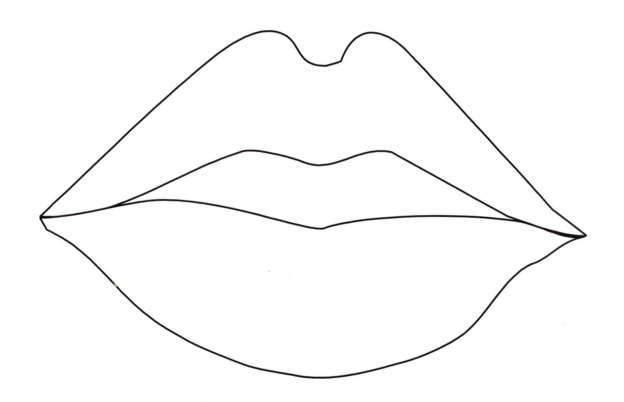

# nose

鼻ㄅㄧˊ 子ㄗ˙
*bi  zi*

*Color the* 鼻子咖啡色

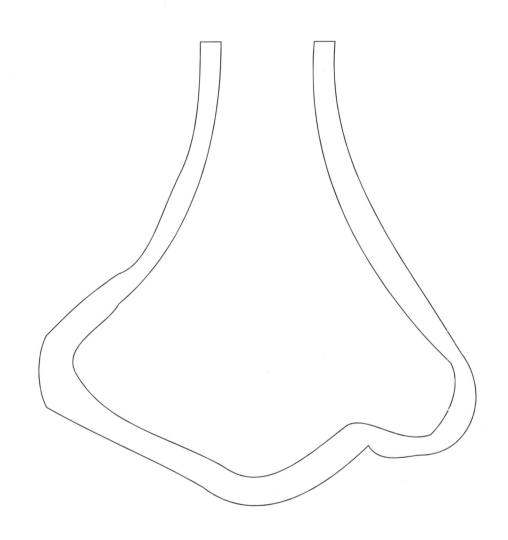

# hair

頭髪
tou fa

*Color the* 頭髪黑色
*Color the bow* 紫色

# hand

手 ㄕㄡˇ
*shou*

*Color the* 手桔紅色

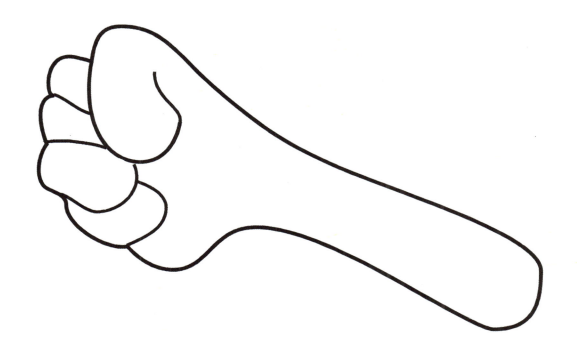

# foot

腳
*jiao*

## *Color the* 腳黃色

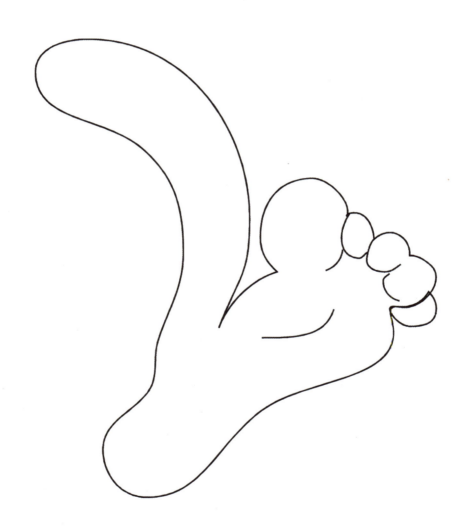

# ear

耳ㄦˇ 朵ㄉㄨㄛ˙
*er  duo*

*Color the* 耳朵綠色

# Match the words to the picture.

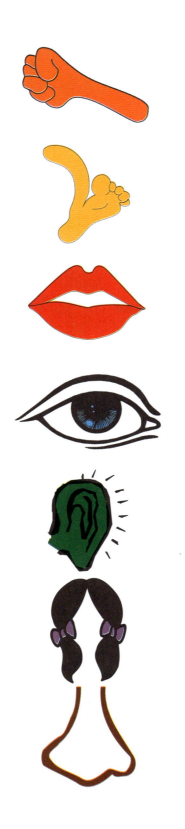

嘴 ㄗㄨㄟˇ　巴 ㄅㄚ
zui　　　　ba

手 ㄕㄡˇ
shou

耳 ㄦˇ　朵 ㄉㄨㄛ
er　　　duo

頭 ㄊㄡˊ　髮 ㄈㄚˇ
tou　　　fa

鼻 ㄅㄧˊ　子 ㄗ
bi　　　zi

腳 ㄐㄧㄠˇ
jiao

眼 ㄧㄢˇ　睛 ㄐㄧㄥ
yan　　　jing

**Look at the picture and read the words aloud.** *When you think you can remember them all turn to the next page.*

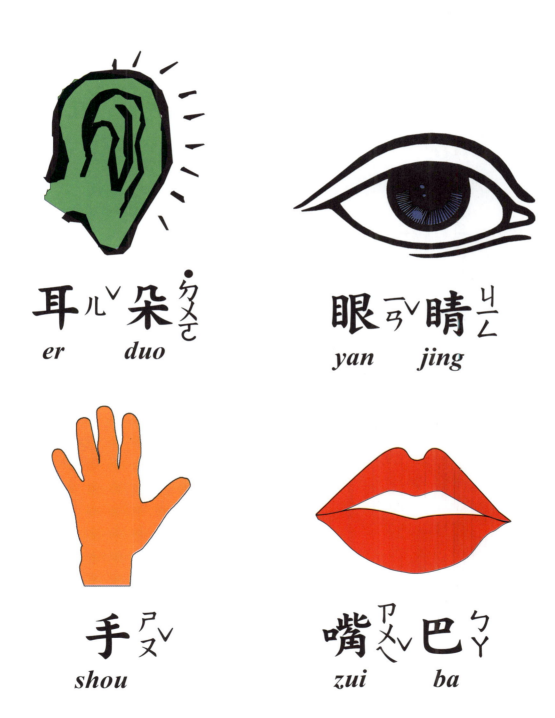

**Find the things you saw on the page before.**
*Circle them.*

腳ㄐㄧㄠˇ
jiao

手ㄕㄡˇ
shou

眼ㄧㄢˇ 睛ㄐㄧㄥ
yan   jing

鼻ㄅㄧˊ 子ㄗ
bi    zi

嘴ㄗㄨㄟˇ 巴ㄅㄚ
zui     ba

耳ㄦˇ 朵ㄉㄨㄛ˙
er   duo

**Look at the picture and read the words aloud.** *When you think you can remember them all turn to the next page.*

頭ㄊㄡˊ 髮ㄈㄚˇ
tou   fa

腳ㄐㄧㄠˇ
jiao

鼻ㄅㄧˊ 子ㄗ
bi   zi

耳ㄦˇ 朵ㄉㄨㄛ˙
er   duo

**Find the things you saw on the page before. Circle them.**

腳 ㄐㄧㄠˇ
*jiao*

手 ㄕㄡˇ
*shou*

眼 ㄧㄢˇ 睛 ㄐㄧㄥ
*yan   jing*

鼻 ㄅㄧˊ 子 ㄗ˙
*bi   zi*

頭 ㄊㄡˊ 髮 ㄈㄚˇ
*tou   fa*

耳 ㄦˇ 朵 ㄉㄨㄛ˙
*er   duo*

# How do you say it in Chinese?
## Circle the right word.

| 腳 jiao | 頭髮 tou fa | 嘴巴 zui ba | 手 shou |  |

| 頭髮 tou fa | 眼睛 yan jing | 鼻子 bi zi | 耳朵 er duo |  |

| 耳朵 er duo | 眼睛 yan jing | 鼻子 bi zi | 嘴巴 zui ba |  |

| 腳 jiao | 手 shou | 眼 yan | 耳 er |  |

| 嘴巴 zui ba | 眼睛 yan jing | 鼻子 bi zi | 頭髮 tou fa |  |

| 手 shou | 腳 jiao | 嘴 zui | 鼻 bi |  |

| 頭髮 tou fa | 耳朵 er duo | 嘴巴 zui ba | 鼻子 bi zi |  |

# Cut and Paste

Cut out the pictures on the bottom of this page and paste them into the right boxes in the puzzle.

| 眼睛 yan gua | 鼻子 bi zi | 嘴巴 zui ba |
|---|---|---|
| 手 shou | 腳 jiao | 耳朵 er duo |
| 頭髮 tou fa | 臉 lian | 身體 shen ti |

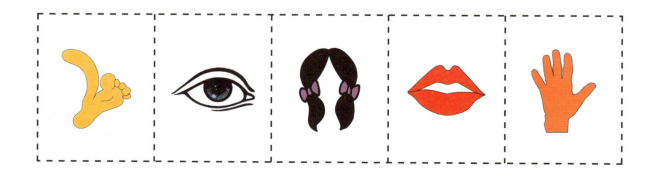

36

**Circle only the pictures mentioned in the box.**

| 手　　眼睛　　鼻子　　嘴巴 |
|---|

# Circle only the pictures mentioned in the box.

| 腳　　眼睛　耳朵　頭髮 |

# Match the words with the things.

     頭髮

     手

     眼睛

     鼻子

     耳朵

     嘴巴

     腳

# Write the correct number for each body part.

1. 嘴巴
2. 鼻子
3. 耳朵
4. 眼睛
5. 手
6. 腳
7. 頭髮

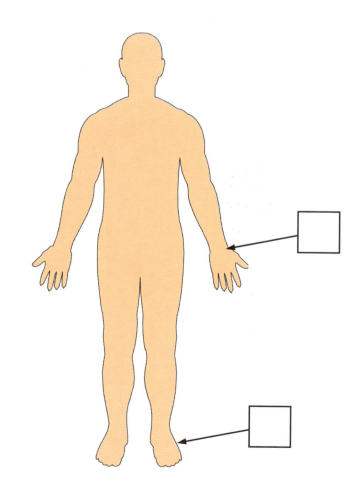

# Below is a list of words hiding in the puzzle. *Find them and circle them.*

(*Words can only be read from left to right or from top to bottom.*)

| 西 | 瓜 | 咖 | 黃 | 六 | 腳 | 嘴 |
|---|---|---|---|---|---|---|
| 巴 | 眼 | 鏡 | 色 | 手 | 紅 | 西 |
| 綠 | 桔 | 子 | 睛 | 藍 | 色 | 黑 |
| 五 | 色 | 十 | 眼 | 睛 | 紫 | 色 |
| 耳 | 朵 | 鼻 | 四 | 九 | 七 | 頭 |
| 子 | 綠 | 子 | 咖 | 嘴 | 巴 | 髮 |

1. Eye
2. Nose
3. Ear
4. Mouth
5. Hair
6. Hand
7. Foot
8. Purple color
9. Black color
10. Blue color
11. Orange
12. Yellow color
13. Nine
14. Five
15. Six

# My Outfit

# clothes 衣ー 服ㄈㄨˊ
## yi fu

**pink color** 粉ㄈㄣˇ 紅ㄏㄨㄥˊ 色ㄙㄜˋ
*fen hong se*

*Color the* 衣服粉紅色

**coat** 外套
*Wai tao*

grey color 灰色
*hui se*

*Color the* 外套灰色

# socks 襪ㄒㄧˋ子ㄗ
## *wa* *zi*

# white color 白ㄅㄞˊ色ㄙㄜˋ
## *bai* *se*

*Color the* 襪子白色

pants 褲子 ㄎㄨˋ ㄗ˙
*ku zi*

long 長 ㄔㄤˊ
*chang*

*long pants* 長褲

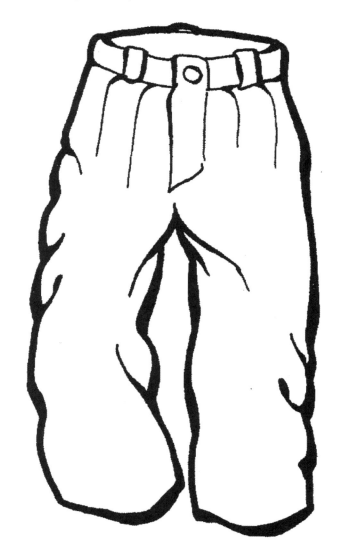

# skirt 裙子 qun zi

# short 短 duan

*short skirt* 短裙

# shorts

短(ㄉㄨㄢˇ) 褲(ㄎㄨˋ)
*duan ku*

# long skirt

長(ㄔㄤˊ) 裙(ㄑㄩㄣˊ)
*chang qun*

長(ㄔㄤˊ) 長長長長長長長
*chang*

短(ㄉㄨㄢˇ) 短短短短短短短短短短
*duan*

| 長 | 長 | 長 |
|---|---|---|

| 短 | 短 | 短 |
|---|---|---|

**hat** 帽ㄇㄠˋ 子 ㄗ˙
*mao zi*

男帽

**male** 男 ㄋㄢˊ
*nan*

女帽

**female** 女 ㄋㄩˇ
*nü*

男 ㄋㄢˊ 男男男男男男
*nan*

| 男 | 男 | 男 | |

女 ㄋㄩˇ 女女女
*nü*

| 女 | 女 | 女 | |

# shoes 鞋(ㄒㄧㄝˊ)子(ㄗ˙)
### xie  zi

 男鞋

女鞋

 大鞋

小鞋

**big** 大(ㄉㄚˋ)
*da*

**small** 小(ㄒㄧㄠˇ)
*xiao*

大(ㄉㄚˋ) 大 大 大
*da*

小(ㄒㄧㄠˇ) 小 小 小
*xiao*

# How do you say it in Chinese?
## Circle the right word.

| 襪ㄨㄚˋ子ㄗ˙ | 帽ㄇㄠˋ子ㄗ˙ | 褲ㄎㄨˋ子ㄗ˙ | 鞋ㄒㄧㄝˊ子ㄗ˙ |
| wa zi | mao zi | ku zi | xie zi |

| 襪ㄨㄚˋ子ㄗ˙ | 帽ㄇㄠˋ子ㄗ˙ | 褲ㄎㄨˋ子ㄗ˙ | 鞋ㄒㄧㄝˊ子ㄗ˙ |
| wa zi | mao zi | ku zi | xie zi |

| 襪ㄨㄚˋ子ㄗ˙ | 帽ㄇㄠˋ子ㄗ˙ | 褲ㄎㄨˋ子ㄗ˙ | 鞋ㄒㄧㄝˊ子ㄗ˙ |
| wa zi | mao zi | ku zi | xie zi |

| 襪ㄨㄚˋ子ㄗ˙ | 帽ㄇㄠˋ子ㄗ˙ | 褲ㄎㄨˋ子ㄗ˙ | 裙ㄑㄩㄣˊ子ㄗ˙ |
| wa zi | mao zi | ku zi | qun zi |

| 襪ㄨㄚˋ子ㄗ˙ | 帽ㄇㄠˋ子ㄗ˙ | 褲ㄎㄨˋ子ㄗ˙ | 鞋ㄒㄧㄝˊ子ㄗ˙ |
| wa zi | mao zi | ku zi | xie zi |

| 衣ㄧ服ㄈㄨˊ | 帽ㄇㄠˋ子ㄗ˙ | 褲ㄎㄨˋ子ㄗ˙ | 外ㄨㄞˋ套ㄊㄠˋ |
| yi fu | mao zi | ku zi | wai tao |

| 衣ㄧ服ㄈㄨˊ | 帽ㄇㄠˋ子ㄗ˙ | 褲ㄎㄨˋ子ㄗ˙ | 外ㄨㄞˋ套ㄊㄠˋ |
| yi fu | mao zi | ku zi | wai tao |

# Match the words to the picture.

   帽子 mao zi

   鞋子 xie zi

   衣服 yi fu

   裙子 qun zi

   褲子 ku zi

   外套 wai tao

   襪子 wa zi

**Look at the picture and read the words aloud.** *When you think you can remember them all turn to the next page.*

**Find the things you saw on the page before. *Circle them.***

外ㄨㄞˋ 套ㄊㄠˋ
wai tao

鞋ㄒㄧㄝˊ 子ㄗ˙
xie zi

褲ㄎㄨˋ 子ㄗ˙
ku zi

裙ㄑㄩㄣˊ 子ㄗ˙
qun zi

襪ㄨㄚˋ 子ㄗ˙
wa zi

帽ㄇㄠˋ 子ㄗ˙
mao zi

**Look at the picture and read the words aloud.** *When you think you can remember them all turn to the next page.*

衣一 服ㄈㄨˊ
*yi    fu*

襪ㄨㄚˋ 子ㄗ˙
*wa    zi*

褲ㄎㄨˋ 子ㄗ˙
*ku    zi*

帽ㄇㄠˋ 子ㄗ˙
*mao    zi*

55

**Find the things you saw on the page before. *Circle them.***

衣 yi　服 fu　　鞋 xie　子 zi

帽 mao　子 zi　　裙 qun　子 zi

褲 ku　子 zi　　襪 wa　子 zi

# How do you say it in Chinese?
## Circle the right word.

| 小ㄒㄧㄠˇ鞋ㄒㄧㄝˊ | 男ㄋㄢˊ鞋ㄒㄧㄝˊ | 女ㄋㄩˇ鞋ㄒㄧㄝˊ | 大ㄉㄚˋ鞋ㄒㄧㄝˊ |
|---|---|---|---|
| xiao xie | nan xie | nü xie | da xie |

| 男ㄋㄢˊ襪ㄨㄚˋ | 女ㄋㄩˇ帽ㄇㄠˋ | 長ㄔㄤˊ褲ㄎㄨˋ | 男ㄋㄢˊ鞋ㄒㄧㄝˊ |
|---|---|---|---|
| nan wa | nü mao | chang ku | nan xie |

| 長ㄔㄤˊ襪ㄨㄚˋ | 大ㄉㄚˋ帽ㄇㄠˋ子ㄗ | 短ㄉㄨㄢˇ褲ㄎㄨˋ | 小ㄒㄧㄠˇ鞋ㄒㄧㄝˊ子ㄗ |
|---|---|---|---|
| chang wa | da mao zi | duan ku | xian xie zi |

| 女ㄋㄩˇ裙ㄑㄩㄣˊ | 男ㄋㄢˊ鞋ㄒㄧㄝˊ | 短ㄉㄨㄢˇ褲ㄎㄨˋ | 衣ㄧ服ㄈㄨˊ |
|---|---|---|---|
| nü qun | nan xie | duan ku | yi fu |

| 小ㄒㄧㄠˇ鞋ㄒㄧㄝˊ | 大ㄉㄚˋ衣ㄧ | 長ㄔㄤˊ褲ㄎㄨˋ | 短ㄉㄨㄢˇ褲ㄎㄨˋ |
|---|---|---|---|
| xiao xie | da yi | chang ku | duan ku |

| 衣ㄧ服ㄈㄨˊ | 長ㄔㄤˊ裙ㄑㄩㄣˊ | 短ㄉㄨㄢˇ裙ㄑㄩㄣˊ | 外ㄨㄞˋ套ㄊㄠˋ |
|---|---|---|---|
| yi fu | chang qun | duan qun | wai tao |

| 長ㄔㄤˊ襪ㄨㄚˋ | 短ㄉㄨㄢˇ襪ㄨㄚˋ | 長ㄔㄤˊ褲ㄎㄨˋ | 短ㄉㄨㄢˇ褲ㄎㄨˋ |
|---|---|---|---|
| chang wa | duan wa | chang ku | duan ku |

# Circle only the pictures mentioned in the box.

| 長ㄔㄤˊ 褲ㄎㄨˋ | 短ㄉㄨㄢˇ 裙ㄑㄩㄣˊ | 女ㄋㄩˇ 鞋ㄒㄧㄝˊ | 小ㄒㄧㄠˇ 外ㄨㄞˋ 套ㄊㄠˋ | 男ㄋㄢˊ 帽ㄇㄠˋ |
|---|---|---|---|---|
| chang ku | duan qun | nü xie | xiao wai tao | nan mao |

# Cut and Paste

**Cut out the pictures on the bottom of this page and paste them into the right boxes in the puzzle.**

| 鞋子<br>xie zi | 裙子<br>qun zi | 帽子<br>mao zi |
|---|---|---|
| 外套<br>wai tao | 衣服<br>yi fu | 長褲<br>chang ku |
| 襪子<br>wa zi | 小鞋<br>xiao xie | 短褲<br>duan ku |

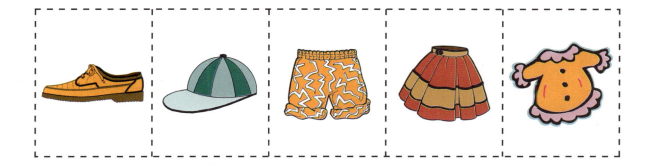

# Color by number

一：紅色　　　　二：紫色　　　　三：黃色

四：桔紅色　　　五：黑色　　　　六：藍色

七：白色　　　　八：灰色　　　　九：粉紅色

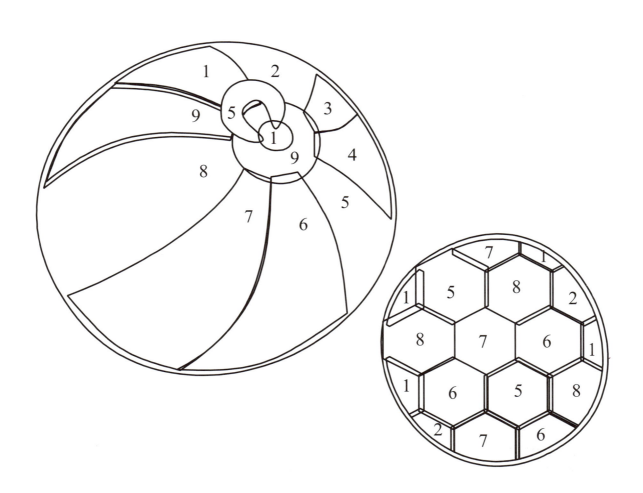

# Fill in the appropriate number in the box.

1. 頭髮
2. 眼睛
3. 鼻子
4. 嘴巴
5. 帽子
6. 鞋子
7. 裙子
8. 腳
9. 衣服
10. 手

# Below is a list of words hiding in the puzzle. *Find them and circle them.*

(*Words can only be read from left to right or from top to bottom.*)

| 短 | 裙 | 長 | 白 | 紅 | 粉 | 女 |
|---|---|---|---|---|---|---|
| 男 | 短 | 褲 | 襪 | 手 | 紅 | 鞋 |
| 外 | 大 | 帽 | 子 | 紅 | 色 | 長 |
| 套 | 耳 | 藍 | 眼 | 睛 | 衣 | 黑 |
| 帽 | 朵 | 灰 | 褲 | 子 | 服 | 頭 |
| 子 | 男 | 鞋 | 小 | 嘴 | 巴 | 髮 |

1. Blue eyes
2. Small mouth
3. Big ear
4. Pink color
5. Female shoes
6. Long pants
7. Short skirt
8. Big hat
9. White socks
10. Shorts
11. Clothes
12. Male coat
13. Grey pants
14. Hat
15. Black hair

# Answers

## page 4
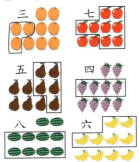

## page 5
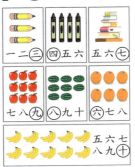

## page 6

## page 14

## page 15
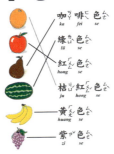

## page 18

## page 20

## page 21

| 七 | 瓜 | 二 | 果 | 葡 | 莓 | 西 |
|---|---|---|---|---|---|---|
| 籃 | 莓 | 蘋 | 四 | 萄 | 草 | 六 |
| 西 | 瓜 | 果 | 萄 | 藍 | 莓 | 三 |
| 五 | 色 | 紅 | 十 | 色 | 黑 | 白 |
| 桔 | 紅 | 色 | 八 | 九 | 色 | 梨 |
| 子 | 綠 | 色 | 咖 | 啡 | 色 | 子 |

## page 30
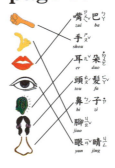

## page 32

# page 34

腳 jiao　　手 shou

眼睛 yan jing　　鼻子 bi zi

頭髮 tou fa　　耳朵 er duo

# page 35

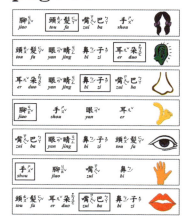

# page 37

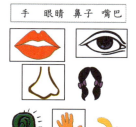

# page 38

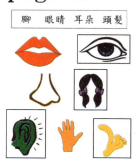

# page 39

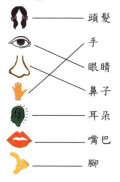

# page 40

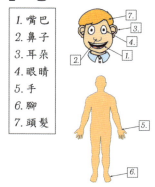

1. 嘴巴
2. 鼻子
3. 耳朵
4. 眼睛
5. 手
6. 腳
7. 頭髮

# page 41

# page 51

# page 52

# page 54

| 外套 wai tao | 鞋子 xie zi |

| 褲子 ku zi | 裙子 qun zi |

| 襪子 wa zi | 帽子 mao zi |

# page 56

| 衣服 yi fu | 鞋子 xie zi |

| 帽子 mao zi | 裙子 qun zi |

| 褲子 ku zi | 襪子 wa zi |

# page 57

| 小鞋 xiao xie | 男鞋 nan xie | **女鞋 nü xie** | 大鞋 da xie | 👠 |
| 男襪 nan wa | 女帽 nü mao | 長褲 chang ku | **男鞋 nan xie** | 👞 |
| 長襪 chang wa | **大帽子 da mao zi** | 短褲 duan ku | 小鞋子 xian xie zi | 🧢 |
| **女裙 nü qun** | 男鞋 nan xie | 短褲 duan ku | 衣服 yi fu | 👗 |
| 小鞋 xiao xie | 大衣 da yi | **長褲 chang ku** | 短褲 duan ku | 👖 |
| 衣服 yi fu | **長裙 chang qun** | 短裙 duan qun | 外套 wai tao | 👗 |
| 長襪 chang wa | **短襪 duan wa** | 長褲 chang ku | 短褲 duan ku | 🧦 |

# page 58

| 長褲 chang ku | 短裙 duan qun | 女鞋 nü xie | 小外套 xiao wai tao | 男帽 nan mao |

# page 61

1. 頭髮
2. 眼睛
3. 鼻子
4. 嘴巴
5. 帽子
6. 鞋子
7. 裙子
8. 腳
9. 衣服
10. 手

# page 62

| 短 | 裙 | 長 | 白 | 紅 | 粉 | 女 |
| 男 | 短 | 褲 | 襪 | 手 | 紅 | 鞋 |
| 外 | 大 | 帽 | 子 | 紅 | 色 | 長 |
| 套 | 耳 | 藍 | 眼 | 睛 | 衣 | 黑 |
| 帽 | 朵 | 灰 | 褲 | 子 | 服 | 頭 |
| 子 | 男 | 鞋 | 小 | 嘴 | 巴 | 髮 |

# Index

**Body parts:**

| | | |
|---|---|---|
| Ear | 耳朵 | /er duo |
| Eye | 眼睛 | /yan jing |
| Hair | 頭髮 | /tou fa |
| Hand | 手 | /shou |
| Foot | 腳 | /jiao |
| Mouth | 嘴巴 | /zui ba |
| Nose | 鼻子 | /bi zi |

**Clothes:**

| | | |
|---|---|---|
| Clothes | 衣服 | /yi fu |
| Coat | 外套 | /wai tao |
| Hat | 帽子 | /mao zi |
| Long pants | 長褲 | /chang ku |
| Long skirt | 長裙 | /chang qun |
| Pants | 褲子 | /ku zi |
| Shoes | 鞋子 | /xie zi |
| Short skirts | 短裙 | /duan qun |
| Shorts | 短褲 | /duan ku |
| Skirt | 裙子 | /qun zi |
| Socks | 襪子 | /wa zi |

**Colors:**

| | | |
|---|---|---|
| Black | 黑色 | /hei se |
| Blue | 藍色 | /lan se |
| Brown | 咖啡色 | /ka fei se |
| Green | 綠色 | /lü se |
| Grey | 灰色 | /hui se |
| Orange | 桔紅色 | /ju hong se |
| Pink | 粉紅色 | /fen hong se |
| Purple | 紫色 | /zi se |
| Red | 紅色 | /hong se |
| White | 白色 | /bai se |
| Yellow | 黃色 | /huang se |

**Fruits:**

| | | |
|---|---|---|
| Apple | 蘋果 | /ping guo |
| Banana | 香蕉 | /xiang jiao |
| Blueberry | 藍莓 | /lan mei |
| Grapes | 葡萄 | /pu tao |
| Orange | 桔子 | /ju zi |
| Pear | 梨子 | /li zi |
| Watermelon | 西瓜 | /xi gua |

**Numbers:**

| | | |
|---|---|---|
| One | 一 | /yi |
| Two | 二 | /er |
| Three | 三 | /san |
| Four | 四 | /si |
| Five | 五 | /wu |
| Six | 六 | /liu |
| Seven | 七 | /qi |
| Eight | 八 | /ba |
| Nine | 九 | /jiu |
| Ten | 十 | /shi |

**Others:**

| | | |
|---|---|---|
| Big | 大 | /da |
| Character | 字 | /zi |
| Female | 女 | /nü |
| Long | 長 | /chang |
| Male | 男 | /nan |
| Short | 短 | /duan |
| Small | 小 | /xiao |

【實用中文】全套共十冊（簡體字版一至四冊已經上市），內容綱要如下：

| | |
|---|---|
| 初級一 | 遊戲學中文——讀、說、聽 |
| 初級二 | 遊戲學中文——讀、說、聽 |
| 第一冊 | 我和我的家人朋友 |
| 第二冊 | 自我介紹（高、矮、胖、瘦…） |
| 第三冊 | 興趣、職業（動物，愛好…） |
| 第四冊 | 日常生活會話（購物，打電話，寫信…） |
| 第五冊 | 文化一：中國的重要節日介紹 |
| 第六冊 | 文化二：中國歷代簡介 |
| 第七冊 | 文化三：中國重要人事物簡介 |
| 第八冊 | 文化四：成語典故介紹 |

§全套十冊各有作業補充練習本和錄音帶，可分別購買。

【遊戲學中文】提供家長和老師 50 個語文遊戲小點子，讓學生在遊戲中學習。

【兒童中文】 "Chinese for Children"
包含著色、找字、連連看、記憶遊戲、剪貼等活動，讓幼兒在遊戲中學習中文，內容包括數字、顏色、水果、身體部位、衣物等。

詳情請洽：創意世界出版社(732) 441-1704 或 e-mail：clincomp@cs.com

**"The Effective Way of Learning Reading, Writing, and Speaking Chinese"** *is a series of ten books for native English speakers. The contents are as follows: (All the books include exercises. )*

**Contents**

| | |
|---|---|
| **For beginners I** | Fun way of Learning Chinese |
| **For beginners II** | Fun way of Learning Chinese |
| **Level I** | My family, my friends and myself |
| **Level II** | Self introduction |
| **Level III** | Interests, occupations, animals |
| **Level IV** | Daily conversation |
| **Level V** | Introduction to the Chinese festivals |
| **Level VI** | Introduction to the Chinese dynasties |
| **Level VII** | Introduction to the Chinese famous people, inventions, and events. |
| **Level VIII** | Introduction to the Chinese idioms and phrases |

**"Chinese for Children"** is specially designed for the young native speakers of English. This book provides various activities such as coloring, word puzzle, and cut and paste, etc.

***For more information please call (732) 441-1704 or send e-mail to clincomp@cs.com***